STEP

BY

STEP

GUIDE TO BUILD

THE TEARDROP TRAILER

TABLE OF CONTENTS

History of the Teardrop Trailer

Teardrop Trailers appeared in the 1930s and became extremely popular in the 1940s after World War II. The Depression ended and the war gave the economy a big boost. US citizens wanted to go on vacation with their families.

The United States developed the road network to make travel easier. The droplet trailer was lightweight and could be easily pulled behind a family car that had an engine that was less than 100 horsepower and in some cases a motorcycle in the 1930s and 1940s.

Most of the original teardrop trailers were made from materials obtained from the surplus market during World War II. The chassis was made of steel U-channels or round steel tubes, and in some cases the wheels were from Jeeps that were scrapped and given new life on a drop trailer. The outer skins were usually made of aluminium fenders from World War II bombers, giving the drop trailers their shiny appearance. Some teardrop Trailers are named Woodsy because of the wooden edges.

The popularity of teardrop trailers lasted into the 1950s. This popularity was driven by the fact that people who wanted to make their own teardrop trailers. It's also what makes teardrop trailers come back now. In the 1950s, Popular Mechanics magazine published teardrop trailers plans in its magazine that many used to make their own teardrop trailers. These plans included a wooden trailer. Many teardrop trailers today are built either on purchased steel trailers or on custom steel trailers.

The popularity of the teardrop trailer began to wane in the late 1950s because Americans wanted tourists to be "bigger and better." In the 1950s, cars grew larger and more powerful, and large mobile homes could be towed than smaller drop-shaped trailers.

With gasoline prices ranging from 10 to 20 cents a gallon, there was little to no concern about towing the camper mileage, resulting in lower "Teardrop Trailer" .

There are several tear drop trailer manufacturers these days, but most of the teardrop trailers are made in small specialist workshops. You won't find many wheeled dealers transporting teardrop shaped trailers.

If you are interested in a teardrop shaped trailers, you have four options. You can buy a new teardrop trailer, buy a vintage teardrop trailer (1930-1950) that has been remodeled, or rebuild it yourself or hire someone to rebuild it for you, or set it up yourself with one of our build. While a lot has changed since the introduction of teardrop trailers on the American freeway, the reasons for buying teardrop trailers today are much the same as they were when your father or grandfather built their teardrops in the family garage. Today, teardrop trailers have become popular because of the small cars we drive and the high price of gasoline.

Teardrop trailers are elegant, aerodynamic and practical. The Teardrop Trailer is a child in the world of motor-homes. They are small, so a teardrop trailer is perfect for one or two people. Teardrop trailers can be towed by any vehicle with a tow bar. The smallest cars like the Chevy Aveo or VW Beetle can easily pull a teardrop trailer with them. Please check with the vehicle manufacturer before towing RVs or trailers. Whether you're a weekend backpacker who loves to spend time with your family, or an avid backpacker who hunts and fishes, or you need an inexpensive way to get around, a teardrop trailer might be the one for you. Teardrop trailers are inverted in the shape of a drop, hence the name "teardrop" and that's why we name it "Teardrop trailer".

STEPS TO BUILD THE TEARDROP TRAILER

The Trailer

Before you do anything, you need a trailer. 4 x 8 or 5 x 8 is what this kit is intended for, But if you are making any additional modifications in size, you can still use this guide As an outline. I prefer 4 x 8 for several reasons. First you need to purchase the materials with 4 x 8, sheets of plywood, 2 x 4's, Etc. Also remember, if you're building your trailer, it's because you're trying to keep costs down. Anything larger than 4 x 8 blows the budget. Also, 5 x 8's are just as easy to assemble with the only difference being an extra foot for additional space.

You can purchase the items from your near store or you can also buy the items online to build the trailer. First of all, you need to weld your frame. If you do buy used teardrop trailer then check the frame rust and check the wheel bearings, maybe they need to be replace and or need to be re-grease. Used trailers bearings need to be degreasing. 46 1/2 inches sleeping area is just shy of a double. 58 1/2 inches is just shy of a queen. 6 feet in length allows 2 feet for your kitchen.

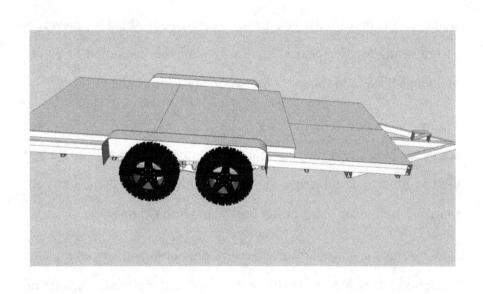

The Trailer Base

Let's begin with a 1/2inch 4 x 8 sheet of plywood. This is pretty straight forward. Make sure it's lined up properly with the frame of the trailer. This is your base. If it's not lined up properly, you will have problems later on down the road. Make sure you use bolts to secure it in place. Every trailer is different in shape so it depends on you what shape you prefer. Once you have secured your sheet of plywood, you're ready for the next step. 2 x 4's and the insulation, if you're building a 5 x 8, add the extra foot wide plywood to the base.

Cut four 2x4s and 461/2 in length (58 1/2 if it's a 5 x 8). Before next step you think about flipping your trailer upside down and spraying it with a rubberized undercoating. You don't have to, but it will give your teardrop trailer the extra protection from all the elements.

Now for the 2 x, 4's and Insulation does not come with any of the kits. Insulation offers support to the Floor. You could replace the Insulation with a couple extra 2 x 4's in the middle of the four - 2 x 4's, To save a little $$$.

Anything to help keep out the heat. Grab the 4 pre-cut 2 x 4's. Space them out across the floor. If you are using Insulation, pre-cut your sheet again to 46 1/2" (or 581/2 for 5x8) then cut each section to fit between the 2 x 4's. Grab the sheet of pre-cut floorboard (46 1/2) (or

58 1/2 for 5x8) and screw the board into the 2x4's. Centre your 2 x 4's between the 4 x 8 sheets. You now have your base. It depends on the size of Styrofoam Insulation, 2 feet, or 4 ft wide and it will be spaced.

The Walls

1. Building the sidewalls was a difficult step. First, you need to create pattern matched interior and exterior walls with the exterior walls being extending 1" lower than the interior walls. To accomplish this step you require measuring, drawing, and checking all the sides. You need to ensure the doors were located at the right place so they wouldn't hit the tire fenders. They were high enough so the walls aligned up perfectly with the floor frame and the slots where the restraining straps would go.

2. Additionally, since the size of the camper body (big curved box) was larger than a single sheet of plywood, and plywood butt didn't seem to overlap on the interior and exterior. This meant you need to overlap the sheets of plywood so the interior had the 8' side of the plywood going vertical and the exterior sides were laid out horizontal.

3. Let's start building the sides by laying out 12 sheets of 1/4" plywood side by side with a 4'x8' side against the 8'x4' side. Laid the plywood out with the two interior finished faces of the sheets facing each other.

4. Then sketch out the desired shape of the camper on the plywood, correcting the profile curves several times until you got the final complete profile.

5. Once you got the profile outlined in pencil then re-drew it with a Sharpie marker because there were several pencil curves in some areas and don't cut the wrong curve. After that laid a cabin door

on the plywood and outlined the cut-out profile as well as outlined the cut-out profile for the back hatch. The doors were difficult so get properly positions and it takes time to adjust.

6. Ensure the doors wouldn't hit the tire wells or anything else when opened. Grab several wood clamps and clamped all the plywood sheets together. Then strategically screwed all the sheets together so they wouldn't move while you were cutting them out.

7. Slid multiple 2"x4"x8' boards under the walls and began cutting using a saber-saw, staying just outside the marked line. Once the outside curves were cut and the scrap wood moved out of the way then drills four (4) 1" holes with a spade bit on the 4 corners of the door outline. Make sure there is a support board under each of the 4 points so the spade bit doesn't tear the final layer of plywood when it pokes through that layer. With the 4 holes drilled, cut the door openings out.

8. When you were completely done with cutting the sidewalls remove the screw used to hold the plywood sheets together and began to take the walls apart. Labelling the pieces as Interior wall 1,2,3,4,5,6, Exterior wall 1,2,3,4,5,6. Labelling the sides that would not be exposed to the interior or exterior of the cabin.

9. The next step was to frame the walls. Many teardrop trailer plans only use 1 or 2 sheets of 3/4" or 1" plywood to provide thickness for the walls. The trailer needs insulation, structural strength, reduced weight, and the ability to run wiring through the walls of the camper.

10. The frame consists of 1"x4" pine boards that were glued and screwed or brad nailed to the walls. Framed out the openings for the doors and where the bulkhead between the interior cabin and

the kitchen would be as well as where the countertop and interior cabinet would be located. The exterior curves were also framed out with 1"x4" boards. Each board was cut with a mitre saw to join together and frame the outer edge of the walls.

11. Once the 1"x4" boards have been mounted and dried, use your sabre saw to trim any wood that isn't flush with the inner wall.

12. Clamp the two interior walls together and sand the edges to make them as close to mirror images as possible. This is the last chance to get two perfect walls.

13. The next step was to determine the location for all the lighting, switches, and wiring necessary to be run before installing the insulation and closing the walls up. Since all the wiring in the walls was 12 VDC, that meant running a + wire (Red) and (Black) wire for each light switch and the fan. Take 2 overhead LED spotlights, ceiling fan, two reading lights (one on each side of the cabin), and LED light strips in the interior of the cabin and 2 exterior lights one by each door. Wire one exterior light and one LED spotlight to switches next to each door. The ceiling fan had its switch so you just need sufficient wire for a home run (1 red and 1 black wire run continuously to the circuit panel). Reading lights with their own integrated switches also requires home runs. Finally the LED strip lights, one strip on each side of the cabin running along with the ceiling. These were controlled by a switch on the interior cabinet.

14. The key thing here is to determine where you want to mount your lights, fans, switches, and run the wires at this stage. Running the wires requires drilling through the 1" x 4" boards pulling pairs or multiple pairs of wires through the holes. It's better to pull an

extra 5 feet of wire (and leave it hanging) at this stage and cut it back later than to only pull 3 feet.

1" x 4" pine boards were glued and nailed (1" brads) to the exterior facing side of each interior wall
The boards overlapped the walls and the door frame and were trimmed back once the exterior walls were glued and screwed on

Foam insulation fills all the gaps - cut to size

Shelf support

Pre-drill all mounting screw holes
Don't drill screw holes where the 2" nylon strap will be used to hold the camper onto the trailer.

Bulkhead, cabinetry, and galley supports

Mounting the walls and roof struts

1. The next step is to mount the interior walls to the floor. To do this use an extension bit and drilled 1/2" holes about halfway through the bottom of the frame. Drill 9 holes on each wall and then use long 3/8" brad point bits to finish drilling through the frame. Next ran a strip of glue along the bottom of one wall and mounted it along the edge of the base frame using 3" #10 screws to hold the wall in place. Repeat the process for the second wall. Then took some of the firing laths and carefully measured the distances between each wall as mounted on the floor and use the firing lath and screws to temporarily hold the walls as parallel to each other as possible while the glue dried.

2. The interior walls are now mounted and you have the wires pulled through the walls. It is time to install insulation. Use 3/4" - 4'x8' sheets for insulation. Measure the space in the wall between the 1" x 4" boards, cut the insulation to size. Cut a fraction larger than measured so the insulation would be a tight fit. Cut grooves in the insulation where the wire was in the walls.

3. Mark where the wires are as you install the insulation both on the insulation and on the 1"x4" boards. This is very important to do so that you don't drive a screw or nail through your wiring later on. As soon as you get the insulation installed.

4. Each wall has been framed with 1x4 lumber has some wiring for future lighting pulled through it has been insulated. Use a sanding process to ensure the edges of the walls are as similar as possible.

5. Next dry-fit the exterior walls and marked them to show where the wiring is so you won't nails or screws in those areas. Additionally, the exterior walls were marked to show where the bulkhead between the cabin and the kitchen goes and where the shelf over the headboard was to be mounted. The exterior walls mounting holes were marked, then drilled and countersunk. Once an exterior wall piece was ready, the glue was applied to the framing and the exterior wall panels were screwed in place.

6. The next step was to mount the bulkhead between the galley and the cabin. This consists of 3 main pieces of 1/2" plywood, two mounted vertically and one horizontally.

7. The bottom piece height was set so it could fully slide a cooler beneath it and still leave room for a 2" shelf above the cooler. Cut the bottom piece to size of approximately 69 3/4" x 28" and mark the location on the floor as well as on interior walls.

8. Use a level to make sure the piece was perpendicular to the cabin floor. Remove the bottom piece and drill mounting holes through the walls from the inside of the cabin, put the bottom piece back in and drill 1/8" pilot holes into the plywood from the exterior. This is followed by running a line of glue around the sides, bottom of the plywood, and use 3" #8 flat head screws. Countersink the exterior walls before using them. For the bottom use 1" brad nails

and secured the bottom of the plywood bulkhead to the cabin floor.

9. The horizontal part of the bulkhead is installed next. Make sure to use a measure at all 4 corners of the plywood to ensure this piece is parallel to the cabin floor.dry fit, mark, remove, drill from the inside, drill from the outside, countersink in the outside, glue the top edge of the bottom bulkhead and the edges of the horizontal plywood, install and screw it together. This is the foundation for the galley tabletop and the bottom of the interior cabinets. This piece of plywood will get a 3/4" wide piece of cherry trim later, so make sure it is at least 3/4" to 1" shy of the back edge of the galley. There will be a galley door that needs to close!

10. The next piece is the final vertical bulkhead. Cut the plywood to 69 3/4" in width and then dry fit it on the horizontal bulkhead moving it forward and back until you got it where it needed to be installed. So there was 2 1/8" to 2 1/4" of clearance. Once you positioned it and marked it for cutting to vertical size then cut and re-fit it.

11. Adding the bulkheads stabilized the side walls. Next, add a couple of vertical partitions in the galley to make three sections.

12. One section to be used for sliding shelves for the propane grill and propane stove, one section for a cutlery drawer, cooler, two -12 VDC batteries, and a plastic container for the pots, pans, misc cooking utensils. The final section was for 2 - 6-gallon containers of water, a drawer with a hole cut in it for a plastic bin to use as a

sink, and to store a couple of hydraulic jacks to stabilize the trailer at night.

13. Next was the installation of the firing lath struts between the two walls. The firing lath must be straight with no knots. Each one was cut individually. The walls tend to warp a little and by measuring the exterior at each point a strut was to be installed. Pull or push the walls in/out by 1/8" to 1/16" of an inch. Each strut was dry fit, predrilled, glue applied, then screwed into place with a single 2 1/2" #8 flat head screw.

14. For the top of the cabin, this process changed a little because a 12 VDC powered roof vent to be installed. To do this use 1"x4" pine lumber to build a mounting hole for the roof vent. Cut 4 - ~69 3/4" x 1" x 4" pine boards mounting two flushes and separate the top edge of the trailer walls by about 12 1/2". Then mount firing lath struts against the outer edges of the 1" x 4" glued and nailed with 2" nails. Cut four boards of 1" x 4" x 12 1/2" and dry fit perpendicular to the long boards. Use the drill to make 2 holes at each end of the short boards, glued, and screwed them to the long boards.

15. The thickness of the 1" boards is closer to 3/4" and the firing lath struts are nominally 2" wide, so sandwiching 2 - 1" by 4" boards together still leaves a slight gap on the underside. To compensate for this cut some strips of 1/4" plywood and used them in between the 1"x4" to gain the thickness needed.

16. **NOTE:** it's really important to run the ceiling fan wiring from the sidewall to the location where the ceiling fan will be wired at this time. If you forget to do it, it'll be really difficult to hide later on.

17. Complete the installation of the struts about every 6" - 12". From where the back hatch is to be installed then stops to mount firing lath struts about 12". The pine firing lath isn't strong enough to handle the mounting of the back hatch hinge. Make two pairs of 3/4" x 2" by ~69 3/4" oak boards and glue them together. Once dry, they were mounted as the final two roofs struts glued and screwed to the sidewalls. Here use two 10 flat head screws of 3".

18. Before completing this stage of the project install 6 - eye bolts along the roofline. The idea was to have mounting points for tarps when stuck camping with heavy rain or to provide for tie-down points for a roof rack in the future. The eyebolts were 4" to 6" long. The eyebolts came in really handy to a tie tarp to during the trip.

The Interior Roof

Install a 2 x 2, also known as a rib, every 2 feet flush with the top of the walls. The last rib is important. Here the inner wall meets flush with the rib and is also the beginning of the rear galley door. There is an additional rib that aligns with the last rib for added reinforcement. Now is the time to get the pre-cut 461/2 inch wide 1/8 inch thick STD hardboard (or 581/2 for 5x8- you will need 2 sheets). If you're building the 5 x 8 you will use white aluminium instead. Take your time, and be patient. The hardboard is very flexible and somewhat fragile. You don't want to break it. Aluminium is flexible and sturdy.

Slide it into the trailer. Remember it's a tight fit. Get underneath it and push it up against the roof until you hit the ribs. Make sure the hardboard is flush from the bottom of the floor to the top of the last rib. If you did it properly, it should look like the picture on the right. Secure the ceiling at the top with 3/4 inch wood screws and the bottom by the floor. Then take a bead of white caulking from top to bottom to seal the floor with the walls and roof. You can also caulk all the areas that the hardboard touches the ribs, making for a solid seal on the roof top.

Interior Ceiling

1. Mounting the interior cabin ceiling was the most difficult part of the entire project. Take some Italian made 1/8" plywood (4'x8' sheet) that was made to flex along the length instead of the width of the plywood. Start by carefully measuring the interior of the cabin width between each wall. The interior width was a nominal 69 1/2" and required nearly 11 feet of plywood, three sheets side by side. The trim nails can be punch through the 1/8" plywood because it was very thin so you need a way to hold the plywood against the frame struts. Before beginning the installation, Cut about 30 pieces of 1/4" - 1" x 12" pieces of plywood and used them as nailing blocks to hold the plywood against struts while the glue was drying.

2. The first piece of installation was easy. From the front cabin floor it went up 4 feet. The curves for this piece were pretty simple and it was easy to install. Cut and verify the piece and dry-fitted it properly. You had to add in two extra struts for the bottom and top of the plywood to be attached to. Load the finish nailed with 1" nails, spread glue on all the struts, pushed the plywood against the struts, and used the nailing blocks to hold the plywood tight against the struts until the glue dried. The second piece was the child problem for the installation. This was a very tight inside curve, it was overhead, and keeping it in place was difficult.

Following the pattern from the last piece, measure, and dry fit then everything seemed to be ok. The problems started when you tried to hold it in place and nail it against the struts. You can take someone's help by placing them inside the cabin to hold the wood in place as you can glue and nailed it tight. The inside curve was too tight and you can crack the plywood about 6 inches up from the seam after this you nail the plywood into place. By this, you had access to the exterior and you will able to layer a couple of layers of the 1/8" plywood on the backside and glue/nail everything together to fix the crack.

3. The 3rd piece went in pretty easily and almost done with the interior ceiling. The final step was to carefully cut out the hole for the vent. To do this use a dermal tool with a fine saw blade and cut from the exterior. This worked pretty well.

4. During this stage, you can also make a shelf - 3/4" x 10" x 70" that was mounted in the front of the cabin. This was placed so it would be convenient to reach up to while laying in bed and put water bottles, reading glasses, books, etc. up for the night. The shelf was trimmed to 69 3/4" to fit in the cabin.

5. The location for the shelf was noted on the exterior cabin walls when they were glued and screwed on, so it was easy to mark, drill, and countersink the holes through the outer wall.

6. The shelf was held in place while the apprentice can use an ice pick to mark where the pilot holes in the shelf were to be drilled.

7. Once the shelf pilot holes were drilled use 3" #10 screws to mount the shelf. Didn't use glue here because the fit was tight and you can get glue on the cabin walls.

8. The final step was to paint the interior ceiling flat white, starting at the shelf at the front of the cabin to the back of the cabin. Tape and cover all the shelving and the walls to prevent drips from ruining any of the interior finish.

Wiring your trailer

1. The camper self-contain two 12 VDC light truck batteries for all electrical needs. Create a wiring closet in the interior of the cabin between the two storage cabinets and a removable drawer.

2. Locate it under the big centre drawer so you could remove the drawer and have sufficient workspace where the wiring was contained.

3. Start with the AC power: Add the ability to connect the campground 120VAC power if it was available then we would use it in the future.

4. The 120VAC was wired to two GFCI outlets and a battery charger - with the battery charger connected to an outlet that was in series with one of the GFCI outlets. The GFCI outlets are being used as the circuit breakers for the camper, in addition to the circuit breakers that are provided by the campgrounds as part of the AC outlets at the sites.

5. Use 12 gauge multi-strand wires for all AC connections.

6. Wiring was pretty simple and easy.

7. 120VAC comes into the cabin through a weatherproof side port. The Ground (Green) goes directly to a wiring block that is common for all the 120VAC outlets.

8. The initial run (neutral - white and hot - black) runs to a 120VAC GFCI outlet in the interior cabin.

9. This GFCI outlet then runs to a standard 120VAC outlet for the battery charger

10. The standard 120VAC outlet is then connected to the galley 120VAC GFCI outlet.

11. Connect the battery charger to the interior outlet and feeds the batteries located in the galley area on the other side of the cabin bulkhead.

12. Separate the entire 12 VDC circuitry from the 120 VAC and with every 12 VDC circuit use fuse separately. Use 18 gauge wires for this circuit.

13. The concept of operation for using two batteries is as follows:

   ❖ Connect the first Battery to the battery charger and when AC power is available the battery is beginning to charge.

   ❖ During this time all lights and the ceiling fan are powered by second.

   ❖ When the charging of the second battery starts dropping (very noticeable when the fan slows down) then swap the connections on the batteries and the second battery starts charging while the first battery provides the 12VDC source.

   ❖ In case no AC power is available then swaps a partially drained battery with the main truck battery and it charges during the day while you were driving around and swap it back out when it's charged. In this way, both batteries are used, but at no time is either battery completely drained.

- ❖ You were able to get nearly 8 days of use out of the combined battery setup without needing to recharge a battery. This included lighting for 3-4 hours every evening and running the ceiling fan for at least 8 hours a night.

14. It will run the following circuits:
    - ❖ Exterior Door Lights
    - ❖ Interior reading lights
    - ❖ Ceiling fan/vent
    - ❖ Interior floodlights
    - ❖ Interior LED strip lights
    - ❖ Galley Hatch LED strip light
    - ❖ Galley Hatch LED floodlights
    - ❖ Interior 12VDC socket
    - ❖ Exterior 12VDC socket

15. It doesn't seem like you need a lot of wiring but remember that each circuit requires a hot (+) and ground (-) wire and that switches need a run from the source than to the appliance (light, outlet, fan). Additionally, all the switches that you use had LED lights on them to find them easier in the dark. Tape off the (+) wires going to the switch for the appliance to light the switch LEDs, but you still had to run the ground wire back to the control panel.

16. When running the wiring through the walls, it's important to mark where the wires are being run so that you don't accidentally put

a finishing nail or screw through the wire at a later time. It is better to use a light pencil for marking on the interior. For the exterior use black permanent markers to mark the no-go zones.

17. Mount the batteries well so the batteries didn't bounce around by themselves in the back of the camper. So use 3 - 1" wide racketing tie-downs. One tie-down for each battery to hold it to the floor of the trailer and then one tie-down to hold both batteries to the bulkhead that separated the living area from the galley area.

18. You can select lighting based on your interest. Purchase 16 feet of exterior LED strip lighting (12 VDC) that was able to cut to size and solder the + and - connections to. The strip lights came with self-adhesive backing and worked out well for installation. Ran a strip along both sides of the interior cabin and connected both strips to a single switch. Ran a single strip over the cabinets in the cabin to provide lights in the storage area. Cut some 3/4" by 3/4" strips of cherry and then removed a 1/2" square out of the wood to leave some L shaped molding that could hide the wiring behind.

19. Mount the exterior door lights next to the door and connect it to the interior switches on both sides of the cabin, just inside the door frame.

20. Mount a pair of reading lights (also LED) on each side of the cabin wall about 30" above the floor. Place an individual switch on each light so all had to run were + and - to each light.

21. Hide the wiring panel behind the middle of the cabinets in the cabin. Connect the + 12 VDC from the batteries to a 12 outlet fuse block to give 12 circuits more. Use crimp-on quick to fuse block for the positive wires.

22. Connect the ground (-) wires to the bottom of the fuse panel. On each ground wire end crimp the spade lugs.

For installing the solar system

About Solar Concept

For installing a solar panel, the solar panel is of 42V or 250W panel. The voltage goes through a Midnight Brat charge controller to a pair of 12V deep cycle batteries. The Brat is a great little charge controller with a lot of options for a small off-grid system. The batteries run a 2500 Watt inverter. The inverter has three 120V outlets and features a pretty low idle current which is important. 2000W or more is required to start and run an air conditioner like the smallest window AC. Waterproofing around the AC unit includes an eyebrow shelf that keeps any leaks out. On two deep cycle batteries, the AC can run all night off-grid.

You can also install an electric oil heater. These are very safe heaters compared to ones with open elements and the outside never gets too hot to touch. The electric heater draws too much voltage to run on solar.

AC cord access hatch allows a cord to go from inside the trailer to an outside source. The AC can run on solar for a night but after then you need to charge up or plugin.

About Solar System Wiring

Wire Size Calculator

The whole point of solar panels on the roof of your mobile home is that they charge the batteries in your home.

They also generate energy that can be used throughout the day when the sun is shining.

Electricity from solar panels is wired to your mobile home, solar regulator and batteries.

Depending on the length of your RV and the location of the solar components, there may be long cables.

The longer it takes to lay the cable (due to the large distances between solar components and batteries), the greater the voltage loss.

In other words, you are losing some of the power the solar panels are generating due to the wiring the power has to travel. This loss is prevented by using larger sized (gauge) wiring but try to avoid using too large of wiring size for some reasons.

Use the right size (Gauge) wire

❖ The larger the size (gauge) wire you use, the more expensive it is per foot (copper is used to making quality wiring - the type you will be using - and copper isn't cheap)

❖ The larger the size (gauge) wires you use the more difficult it is to install (thicker wires take up more space and is harder to 'shove' through the holes it has to run through)

❖ Larger diameter (gauge) wire is heavier, and weight is a consideration for most RVs.

Voltage Drop Calculator

To properly use the voltage drop calculator you will need to know the following:

❖ Calculate Vmp (voltage) of the solar panels based on if they are wired in series or parallel

❖ amp (amps) of the solar panels (calculated based on if they are wired in series or parallel)

❖ The distance each wiring run is going to travel

Laying Out an RV Solar System

Before you can start spending your hard-earned money on solar components, you need to know where things will go.

By this you get an idea about how many solar panels will fit on the roof of your RV, and how much wire you will need to purchase to join everything up.

Mapping the RV's Roof

The first step was to map out the roof of the trailer. You have to see how much space (and what shape space was) you have to work with. Climbed up on the roof armed with a long measuring tape and a pad of paper, then sketched the rough location of whatever was on the roof that would get in the way of the solar panels.

(Air conditioner, roof vents, TV antenna, etc.)

Measured the distance (and size) of each item from the edges and the front and rear of the RV.

The usable area on the roof was also measured so you know how much total area the roof had.

Once back on the ground transfer all these measurements to a clean piece of paper.

The idea is to decide that one square on the graph paper represents 'X' number of inches in the real world.

Then draw out the rectangular shape of the roof, to scale, as a starting point.

Add all existing roof elements (again to scale) in the correct places according to your dimensions.

As a result, you will get a large-format drawing of your roof with all the obstacles that you need to avoid when installing solar panels.

Then cut out scale mock-ups of the solar panels considering using to figure outplacement.

You need to take into consideration the shading of the solar panels by taller objects on your roof, such as the air conditioner.

How many Solar Panels and where

You can settle 600 watts of rooftop solar which meant three 200 watt panels.

It includes two rectangular-shaped panels along with a single square panel and best to fit on the roof. You need to be flexible as you do your solar install.

Things will come up that you didn't anticipate and you will always end up having to make more runs to the hardware store than expected. Get the Wires from the Roof into the RV. You can run the wires from the roof into the rig via the rooftop refrigerator vent.

This eliminated the need to punch another hole in the RV's roof. Use the MC4-Y connector to combine wires from two rectangular solar panels into a single set of cables that go through the roof and fridge radiator opening. This avoided additional cables both on the roof and in the air vent.

This meant four wires (two wires from the rectangular solar panels and two wires from the square panel) went through roof vent to mount the combiner box right inside the rig.

Where to Put the Solar Controller?

Put the solar controller close to the RV's batteries. You can install the solar controller in the forward baggage compartment, which is close to the batteries while being protected from the weather.

Always try to use lithium batteries. Putting the lithium batteries here served two purposes:

1. They are out of the elements and secure from theft.
2. They were as close to the solar controller as possible.

Where to Run the Wires?

The general idea was to get the wires from the solar panels on the roof, through the roof, into some sort of a combiner, down under the belly of the trailer (belly isn't enclosed), forward to the solar7 controller (which means back up through the belly), down from the solar controller through the belly again, forward to the batteries.

Once the wires were through the roof then run them straight down the pantry and through the floor.

Drill a hole in the floor that had enough space to run two more wires.

Battery Monitor

The battery monitor is a mandatory piece of equipment with any solar installation. This is because without a battery monitor you cannot know for sure if your batteries are being charged completely each day by your solar system.

Furthermore, you have no idea how much power you use on a typical day.

A battery monitor is a key piece of equipment for any solar installation.

Battery monitor does the following things:

- ❖ It simply monitors the flow of power in and out of the battery.
- ❖ It keeps track of how many amp-hours of power leave the battery and how many are put back in.
- ❖ It also does things like monitor battery voltage and temperature (if you have an optional temperature sensor).
- ❖ It can relay this information back to the solar charge controller via Bluetooth.
- ❖ When installing a battery monitor, make sure there is no load between the shunt and the battery.
- ❖ If there is a load between the shunt and the battery, the shunt won't be able to 'read' it and the battery monitor will not 'record' this load.
- ❖ You may need to move some ground wires around and install a distribution block to allow for this.

General Wiring Concepts

Wiring is the most critical component of solar installation.

Power generated by the solar panels is 'transported' from the panels to the solar controller, and then via wiring to the RV's house batteries.

What Size Wire to Use?

Using cheap and too small of a gauge (diameter) of wire that doesn't use copper strands then you will inhibit the 'flow' of power.

You'll have a solar system that will not be performing as expected and you will be like a sad panda.

To achieve a little voltage drop, you may end up needing a large gauge wire.

It depends on both the length of a wire run and the ampere your solar system can produce.

Using large gauge wire may arise several issues. If you look online, you will get people saying all sorts of percentages of voltage drops are OK, but you want to stick in the low single digits.

Use wiring that gave you a 2-3% voltage drop on some runs, and a lower voltage drop on other runs. A 1% voltage drop potentially means using a rather large wire size (diameter).

Use 4 AWG wires from the solar panel wiring combiner to the solar controller.

Many solar regulators only accept wires that are no larger than 6 AWG (which is less than 4 AWG).

Cut the 4 AWG wire so it fits into the 6 AWG hole in the solar controller.

From the solar controller to the batteries use 4 AWG here as well (or even 2 AWG wire).

Again trim the diameter to allow it to fit into the solar controller output terminals.

Note that this may be too good for your particular setup.

Use a voltage drop calculator to find out what your home needs.

This wire size is probably only needed if you have a large solar panel or a long mobile home (which requires long wiring).

Do Calculations Based Upon Max Capacity

You want to calculate the size of the wires based on the maximum wattage of your solar controller.

This also applies if you are not currently using the full power of the controller.

You should consider possible future expansion of the system (unless you run out of space for solar panels on the roof).

Keep in mind that if you have not already done so, you may want to add ground deployment features (portable panels) in the future.

Ground Deploy Solar Panels

Use your solar controller to carry out ground operations so that the two controllers do not work against each other. When calculating the wire size, be sure to consider the wattage of the grounding plate. When dimensioning your solar controller, take into account the additional power consumption for each use on the ground.

Wire Size to Use

For 24 feet RV needs 'only' 600 watts of solar on the roof (and no plans to ever expand).

You have to use the sized wiring in case of you have a longer RV (which, most likely, will result in longer wiring runs) and/or are installing more solar. This is the wiring size used on solar installation:

- ❖ From the solar panels to the combiner use 10 AWG
- ❖ From the combiner to the solar controller use 6 AWG
- ❖ From solar controller to batteries use 6 AWG

Use welding cable (high-quality copper, very flexible) for the 6 AWG runs and 'solar panel' cable (UV, weather, and corrosion resistant) for the 10 AWG runs on the roof.

Use Quality Wires

For wiring between the combiner box, the solar controller, the controller, and batteries you will want to use welding cable.

You will need welding cable that comes in the larger diameter.

It's highly flexible and is made with pure copper strands.

For the wiring from each solar panel to the combiner box, you will want to use a UV resistant cable called 'tray cable'.

Along the roof of rig your wiring will be run.

Therefore it needs to be able to withstand the sun's UV rays.

Disconnect Switches

To disconnect the solar panels electrically from the solar controller as well as to disconnect the solar controller electrically from the batteries you need disconnect switches. We did this with surface-mount circuit breakers. Use a 30-amp breaker between the solar panels and the controller (because the solar panels could, theoretically, produce no more than a little fewer than 30 amps).

Install a 40 amp circuit breaker between the solar controller and the batteries (the solar controller we used can output 30 amps maximum, so we went with the next size up).

Also, put a 15-amp fuse (via an MC4 in-line fuse holder) at the 'Y' connector that combined the two rectangular solar panel wires and at the square panel (for a total of two fuses).

This isolated the panels in case they had shorts.

Catastrophic Fuse

You need to have a catastrophic fuse right at, or very close to the battery bank.

This protects the wiring in case there is a direct short to ground on the positive wiring from the battery.

If you don't have a safety fuse and no positive ground lead somewhere between the battery and your distribution panel, things go wrong quickly.

An RV battery bank is capable of producing some serious ampere output in a very short amount of time.

There will be some arcing and sparking (to say the least).

The catastrophic fuse is there to prevent this from happening.

If a major positive cable somehow gets grounded, the fuse will 'pop'.

Because it is right at the battery (in other words, it will 'carry' the entire max load of the RV), this fuse is rather large.

Your RV may require a larger fuse. Catastrophic fuse is already present in your RV, and it may be sufficient (depending on its capacity, location, etc).

Use Quality Hardware and Properly Attach

It is next to impossible to purchase pre-made cables in the exact length you need, in the quantity, you will want.

Plus, it may not be possible to run a pre-made cable (with big wiring lugs on the ends) through some spots in your RV as you snake the wiring through your rig.

You will be getting familiar with properly installation of wiring lugs (end connectors).

Use quality wiring lugs and attach them properly.

I recommend using a mechanically connected wire lugs.

If you are going to use solder lugs use fusion lugs for the larger sized wiring that come with solder and flux in the barrel already.

You are going to want to use an anti-oxidant compound when assembling the wire lugs onto the wire.

Apply to the wire end (rub it in) and put a little into the lug itself before crimping.

Lastly, use high-quality adhesive heat shrink that is color-coded (red for positive and black for negative wires).

The adhesive that it inside the heat shrinks will 'ooze' out and create a corrosion-resistant barrier.

Combiner Box

Each solar panel has two wires (positive and negative).

These cables must run from the roof to your installation and ultimately to the solar controller.

Instead of running 6 wires for 3 solar panels from the roof to the solar controller, the idea is to bundle the solar panel wiring into a pair of larger gauge wires. This means you have less wires for a (possibly) long run.

You use some sort of a combiner that allows you to consolidate the 6 wires into 2 wires.

The wires running into the combiner (from the solar panels) are smaller gauge wires and the two wires running out of the combiner are larger gauge wires.

Types of Combiner Boxes

Solar boxes are usually installed on the roof in the middle to limit the length of the wires (routes) from all solar panels to it.

A hole is then drilled in the roof to allow the wires to run from the adder unit to your installation and ultimately to the solar controller.

You can buy a ready-made totalizer box or make one yourself with the power distribution units housed in a weatherproof box.

If you make your own, you have to use the proper method to weatherproof the holes drilled into the box that allow wires to pass through.

For smaller rigs (that don't require long wire runs from the solar panels to the combiner), you may be able to put the combiner inside.

This eliminates the need to have a weatherproof combiner, though you still need a weatherproof method to get the solar panel wires inside.

Solar Charge Controller

Solar controller is to be considered as the heart of any solar installation.

It converts the energy produced by the rooftop (and ground deploy if you are using them) solar panels into something that is used to charge your RV's batteries (and to supply 12-volt electrical power used during the day).

The solar controller was the single most expensive item in solar installation.

What Size Controller?

You want to 'size' your solar controller based on the amp rating (amps) of the solar panels you use.

In any ground deploy panels that you may be using remember that factor (currently, or in the future).

Voltage rating (voltage) will also factor into your charge controller selection, as a controller will have a max input voltage it can handle.

Whether you wire your panels in series or parallel will determine the actual Voltage number you will use when determining charge controller sizing.

Your solar controller wants to be able to handle the maximum amperes that your solar panels (roof and floor) can produce.

Again, this is the amperage of your modules, the sum of which is calculated based on whether you connect your solar modules in series, in parallel, or a combination of both.

Keep in mind that you will probably never see this maximum ampere power from your solar panels as it is based on an ideal scenario.

The ideal scenario would be ideal temperature, ideal tilt angle of the sun, perfectly clean panels, etc., etc.

This means that if you are on the fence with the size of the controller you need (calculations indicating that you could jump one size up), you may be OK with the smaller size.

There is sometimes a significant difference in price for the next size solar regulator, but it is also wise to think about the future. If you plan to install more solar energy in the future, you may still need a larger solar controller.

But if you are on the fence, consider that some solar controllers can 'accept' more than their rated amperage input.

They just can't 'do anything' with those extra amps - they are essentially wasted.

Finally, keep in mind any future possible expansion of your solar setup.

If you have more rooftop space for solar panels, the first thing you should consider is a solar controller that can handle additional modules.

You may want to do a theoretical max solar input calculation based upon how many panels could fit on your roof and initially purchase a solar controller capable of handling this much power.

Solar Controller Location

If you use an MPPT solar controller, then the controller can deliver more amps than it consumes. This means that you want the wiring from the solar controller to the battery to be as short as possible. This minimizes the size of the cable required and the voltage drop (energy loss).

If possible, place the solar regulator near the batteries.

But this isn't always possible, especially if your batteries are hanging out in the open on the tongue of your trailer.

Solar Controller Sensors

The MPPT solar controller that you will be installing is a 'smart' controller.

This means it's able to adjust how long it's charging in each of its charge modes based upon battery condition (voltage) at the beginning of the day.

Parameters such as battery temperature and voltage can also be displayed during the charging process.

A smart solar controller relies on sensors to find out what's wrong with batteries.

This includes voltage and temperature sensors.

The battery monitor can sense battery voltage and temperature.

The battery monitor communicates with the solar controller via a Bluetooth network.

That way, the solar controller knows exactly what's going on with the battery.

This allows the controller to compensate for any voltage drop between it and the battery, as well as to know if the battery is hot and cut back on the charging if so.

Solar Panel Selection

Solar panels come in all different shapes, sizes, styles, power outputs, etc.

The first rule of thumb is that you will want to match all of the solar panels in your system (including ground deploys, if you are using them) as closely as possible when it comes to Vmp and amp ratings.

It will depend on you that whether you're wiring panels are in series, parallel, or a combination of both.

You can use different watt panels in your solar array, but there are a few things to consider:

❖ If you are wiring two+ panels in series (to increase the overall voltage), you will want to match the watt of these panels (or more specifically, the amp rating). Panels wired in series will have their amperage (amp rating) reduced to the lowest amp of the string.

❖ If you aren't wiring panels in series, then you can mix and match solar panel watt rating. They do need to have the same (or very close) Vmp ratings.

Solar Panel Voltage

Ideally, you want to use a higher voltage panel (28+ volts Vmp rating) in your system.

However, high voltage panels are usually quite large and may not have enough space on the roof. An alternative is to use lower voltage panels and connect them in series to achieve higher voltage.

This will require you to have an even number of panels.

MPPT solar controllers perform best when they receive a voltage input of between 2 and 2.5 times nominal battery voltage (for a 12-volt system, nominal voltage is 14 volts).

Highest voltage isn't efficient, so hit the sweet spot if possible.

For a 12-volt system, the ideal Vmp rating would be in the 28-35 volt range (again, this can be achieved by wiring panels in series if possible).

Series or Parallel Solar Panel Wiring

If your solar array has multiple solar panels, you need to decide how they will be connected in parallel, in series, or in combination.

There are pros and cons to each method:

* ❖ When wiring solar panels in parallel, the amperage (amp) rating will combine, but voltage (Vmp) won't.
* ❖ Voltage (Vmp) will be limited to the lowest Vmp rating of an individual panel (thus why it's important to match Vmp as close as possible).
* ❖ When wiring solar panels in series, the voltage (Vmp) will combine, but the amperage (amp) won't.
* ❖ Amps (amps) are limited to the smallest amperage of the individual panel (so do not daisy-chain a 160W panel with a 240W panel as the amperage will be reduced to a 160W panel. The extra watts / amps are "wasted" on a 240W panels.
* ❖ The series connection of solar modules increases the voltage of this chain without increasing the current strength.
* ❖ This allows you to use smaller cables for home work or extend the life without increasing the size of the wire.

As explained above, MPPT controllers like higher voltage inputs, so this could be a good thing.

Solar Panel Shading

One thing to consider when deciding where to place your solar panels on the roof of your RV is shade.

Take a look at other items on the roof (air conditioner, TV antenna, roof vents, etc.) and think about how they cast shadows on your solar panels.

Shadows are bad because even a small shadow spot significantly reduces the output power.

Not only things on the roof can shade the solar panel, but also trees.

Don't park in the shade of trees and expect your mobile home's solar system to generate a lot of energy.

Panels wired in series will all be affected if only one of the panels is shaded.

Panels connected in parallel will only dim the panel with reduced power. When you connect panels in series then the total panel voltage increases. This may be fine for an MPPT controller, but you will have more problems with panel dimming which affects solar performance. Connecting panels in parallel means less dimming issues that affect overall performance, but you cannot increase the overall panel voltage.

If you have an even number of panels (say 4 or 6), then you can use a combination of series and parallel wiring to take advantage of the increased voltage, yet limit the shading effects.

Remember, when wiring solar panels in series, you need to match the amperage (amp) rating (which means use the same wattage panels in a series string).

The amp rating of a string will be the lowest amp rating for a single panel in the string.

You can use a combination of series and parallel wired panels in a solar array, but 'parallel rules' apply at the combiner box, as each string of panels will be wired in parallel at the combiner.

Parallel Rules

❖ The Current (amp) of each string will be added together
❖ Voltage (Vmp) of combined strings will be limited to the lowest Vmp of a string
❖ Restating the above point: Make sure the voltage (Vmp) of each string is the same as one string with a lower Vmp will 'bring down' all other strings (Vmp will be reduced to lowest Vmp of all strings)

Miscellaneous Solar Panel Installation Notes

Listed below are some points about mounting solar panels to the roof of your RV:

- ❖ If you have a fiberglass roof, use 3M VHB tape or 3M Fast Cure 5200 Marine Adhesive to help secure the solar panel mounts to the roof.

- ❖ Use stainless 1 -inch #10 or #12 screws to secure solar panel mount to roof. Always use the appropriate type of caulk for your roof material. You only need to use one screw per leg if your roof can use tape or adhesive (it's a fiberglass roof), otherwise use two screws. Aim for roof trusses/studs so that the screws have something to 'bite' into.

- ❖ Secure the solar panel wiring to the roof every 3 to 5 feet with puddles of sealant (use the correct type of sealant for your roofing material). After drying, apply more sealant to the puddle.

- ❖ It's OK to use MC4 connectors ('Y' branch connectors) to combine solar panel wires to make a home run (wired in either series or parallel depending on how you do things).

PROPEX HEATER

The Propex is air space heaters fuelled by propane or butane. Air for combustion is taken from outside and heat is transferred inside the van via a heat exchanger. It is safe to use without having to vent the inside of the van and the blown heat is dry. Some key features are given below:

- ❖ 6500 BTU
- ❖ Consumption of Propane: In every three hours 1 lb (That's close to 60 hours run time for a 20 lbs propane tank. The heater doesn't run all the time, so we should get a few weeks out of a tank)
- ❖ Electrical Consumption: 1.6 amp

The heater is controlled by a thermostat and cycle ON/OFF to maintain the desired temperature. There is only one speed, so the Propex cycle is larger than the Webasto / Espar cycle (they have 3 speeds, so they run at "low" speed without changing too often). However, the start cycle of the Propex is quieter and doesn't draw as much electrical current as the Webasto/Espar.

Types of Propex heaters
(HS2000 VS HS2211)

HS2000 and H211 are the two types of propex heater and both units are almost identical (BTU, consumption, etc). The only difference between them is that the HS2000 must be installed inside the vehicle while the HS2211 is designed to be mounted outside (or inside). The main differences are stated below:

HS2000

- ❖ Must be installed inside.
- ❖ Must be installed horizontally.
- ❖ Requires passing the combustion intake/exhaust pipes through the floor (in addition to the propane line, if your tank is mounted outside): that's two ~1in diameter holes.

HS2211

- ❖ Can be installed inside or outside.
- ❖ Can be installed on any of its wide or narrow faces, but not nose up or down.
- ❖ If installed outside, the hot air / cold air ducts have to pass through the floor (in addition to the electrical wires): that's two ~ 2.75in diameter holes.
- ❖ HS2211 is slightly quieter than the HS2000.

FOR INSTALLING

Step 1: Material Needed

❖ Propex HS2000 Heater with installation kit

❖ Two-stage propane regulator

❖ 1/4" Propane Copper Tubing

❖ A tube for connecting the tube to propane system then hardware fittings are required for connecting

❖ Ring Terminals

Step 2: Drill Holes for Combustion Intake and Exhaust

Firstly drill the holes. Drill very small pilot holes to confirm that it's clear under the van floor. If you mess up, it's easier to plug small holes.

Drill the hole through the floor slightly larger than the pipe diameter and seal it with High-Temperature RTV (Red) Silicone along the pipe throughout the whole depth. Exhaust pipe gets HOT; it could melt the insulation around if you have some.

Step 3: Install Combustion Intake and Exhaust

Secure the combustion intake and exhaust pipe of the unit using worm gear hose clamps. Make sure it's nice and tight.

Step 4: Route Combustion Intake and Exhaust

Routing requirements to follow:

➤ The combustion intake and exhaust pipes should not be trimmed to ensure that the combustion is balanced and that the unit function properly in the long run.

➤ The combustion exhaust pipe should have a constant downward slope: this is because condensation forms in the pipe and will block the airflow if it's not evacuated.

➤ The combustion exhaust pipe must drain off the edge of the car: carbon monoxide is heavier than air and collects under the car. In this case, carbon monoxide can enter the vehicle through the floor (not completely sealed) and through the floor vent (if available). Safety first!

➤ The combustion intake and exhaust pipes should be 0.5 meters apart: this is to prevent exhaust air from re-circulated into the intake pipe (the unit will malfunction in the long run).

Step 5: Route/Install the Propane Line

The HS2000 contains a compression fitting to connect the 1/4" propane copper line to the heater, so you will have to purchase all the remaining fittings and the copper line to hook it up to your existing propane system.

Some of the propex heater fittings require thread paste (or gas specific Teflon tape), some have to be installed dry, some require an olive and compression nut. Propane is harmful so it is highly recommended a visit to your local hardware store to get help from someone qualified.

Any installation (each fitting and connections) must be tested for leaks with a solution of soap and water.

Step 6: Installation of Hot and Cold Air Ducts

Hot Air Outlet Location

The maximum number of hot air outlet is 3; the total combined length of ducting is no longer than 5 meters and the maximum length to the first outlet should not exceed 1.5m.

Keep in mind that, as opposed to a house, heat is not as uniform in a van: there are cold spots, drafts, etc. So hot air outlet location is important and the "best" location is different from a layout to another. Under-the-passenger-seat is not an option as it's already taken by the Webasto, so we chose to install it at the opposite location of the Webasto hot air outlet, near the garage.

Wrap the hot air duct in Reflectix so it's become colder to the touch.

Fabricate a "double-floor" to route the duct. This creates some additional storage room too!

Cold Air Outlet Location

The cold air intake must be at the bottom of the cab, on a sliding door, etc. If the Propex and the air intake are installed in a cabinet or confined space, be sure to add a vent in the cabinet so that the heater can blow air! Also make sure that hot air does not circulate in the cold air inlet.

Step 7: Install the Thermostat Controller

It should be installed between waist and shoulder level, at a location where there is no cold draft and not too close to the hot air outlet; this is to ensure a proper room temperature reading. The thermostat controller is connected to the heater with a 6-pin plug and the controller is attached to the wall with two screws.

Step 8: Connect the Heater to 12V Power

Before connecting the 12V power supply, the thermostat regulator must be installed first. Otherwise, the heater will blow the internal fuse and become unusable (motherboard must be replaced!)

Note: A 5 amp fuse is required at the fuse block.

Step 9: Fire!

Before starting the unit always turn on the propane. If not, you could get a "Gas Lockout" fault and the gas lockout procedure has to be performed

Gas Lockout Procedure:

➢ First, rotate the temperature knob to MAX.

➢ Then turn the control knob from the FLAME position to the OFF position and then back to the FLAME position.

➢ The complete switching sequence must be completed within 2.5 seconds so that the lock can be released successfully.

➢ The heater can take several attempts before it switches on if there is air in the gas line (e.g. after replacing the gas cylinder).

FOR MAKING CABINETS

➤ Cabinets were started by creating the face frames first - these had to align at the top with the oak strut that was installed to support the back hatch. The top and bottom of the face frame were cut to 69 3/4" long and 10 stiles were cut to 24" long.

➤ Kreg pocket screws were used to connect the horizontal and vertical face frames.

➤ Then connect the face frame to the cabin walls and the galley countertop. Measure, measure, and measure for this installation. The face needs to be perfectly flat for the doors to fit properly and parallel to the cabin bulkhead behind it.

➤ After installing the face frame then cut two pieces of plywood to fit behind the two centre stiles. As the plywood was dry fit then cut the 4 pieces of cherry plywood to cover the plywood. After that glue the cherry plywood and clamped it. Leave it for some time to dry.

➤ There are 3 separate cabinet areas. Split the centre cabinet area into two in a later step. For now, install the cherry plywood made in the prior step was so each piece was flush to the centre cabinet area.

➤ The back of each cabinet area must be measured and a piece of cherry plywood to glue and nailed with brads to it.

- The bottom of the side cabinets was also covered with cherry plywood cut to size.
- Then after this cut the next two shelves from plywood one for each of the side cabinets.
- Glue strips of cherries (1/4-inch thick) and nail them to the cabinets with the top supporting the plywood shelves. Cover 1/2 "plywood shelves with 1/4" cherry plywood.
- With the shelves in place, install the two more stiles using pocket whole joinery to split the cabinets to support the cabinet doors.
- Now the shelves were covered with cherry trim.
- With 220 grit sand and seal the cabinets as well as sides of the galley. It will become easier to clean up any squeeze out from installing the tile adhesive or the tile grout.
- With the cabinet frame complete it's time to install the galley countertop. You need 10 pieces of 12" x 12" black granite tiles but purchase a couple of extra pieces in case you screwed up during the cutting or installation process.
- Start by laying out the full sheets of tiles side by side at the front edge of the galley countertop. Once they are laid out, centre them so there is an equal distance on each side of the tiles to the cabin wall.
- Mark the location of the tiles as centred and then measure for the left and right side cuts. A single tile should yield both sides. Remember when cutting tiles you want to keep the good edge against the other tiles and the edge you cut goes against the cabin

walls or the cabinet frame. Measure this cut a couple of times to get it right before doing any cutting.

➢ Once the front row of tiles is in place start measuring the back row tiles and cut them to fit. The final cuts will be the left and right corner cuts. They will use a full tile between them.

➢ Once everything has been dry fit and fits correctly, remove the tiles.

➢ Purchased a couple of caulk tubes of tile adhesive rather than getting a small bucket of adhesive. Squirt the adhesive on the galley top and spread the adhesive using a cheap plastic tile trowel that you could dispose of when done.

➢ Place back the tiles into their positions starting at a back corner, working across the back, and then adding the front row. Tape all the tiles into place using a piece of wood that had been wrapped with old carpeting to make it 3 or 4 inches thick.

➢ Once the adhesive was dry install the front cherry trim (this piece was sanded and sealed before installation).

➢ For grout, purchase a single tube of grout tinted black and applied it according to the manufacturer's instructions. Only use about a quarter of the tube.

➢ Cleanup was pretty easy since you had already sealed all the wood surrounding the tiles. Now just carefully sponged anything that got on the wood off. Take the precaution of using blue painters tape on all exposed wood but when you peeled the tape off there were a couple of places it has seeped under the tape.

➢ The centre cabinet was split horizontally into a space to store paper towels and a wine rack to hold 3 bottles.

➢ Cut the small piece of the cherry plywood to fit in the centre cabinet that was tall enough to mount the 120VAC outlet and some light switches. Once you had the plywood properly sized in length and the electrical hardware was installed and wired then mount a couple of pieces of scrap wood to the sides of the cabinet to attach the plywood to.

➢ Cut a 3/4 x 2 x 10 piece of cherry and drill the two pocket holes on each end of the wood and attached it above to the outlet box.

➢ Install some shelf supports (1/4-inch thick strips of wood) and cut off a piece of cherry plywood to form the top of the small box where the electrical components were installed.

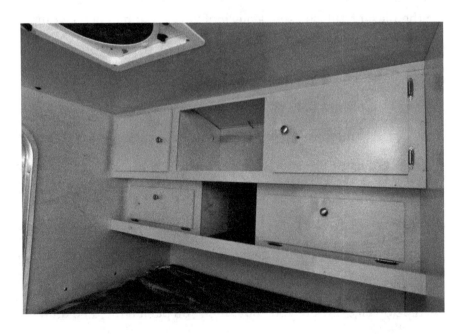

FOR MAKING INTERIOR CABIN

➤ Made the interior cabin face frames with the same materials the galley frames were made of. They are in the same height and don't have a centre stile for the doors to close on though, which makes these cabinets appear larger. They also have no shelves - these cabinets were meant for clothes, towels, bedding, etc.

➤ Start of the cabinet with just the bottom shelf that was installed when the sidewalls were installed and also serves as the galley countertop on the other side of the bulkhead.

➤ Cut two pieces of 1/2" plywood - 24" wide by 30" long and installed them to separate the bottom shelf into 3 sections - 2 - 24" and one 20" centre section.

➤ Marked on the bottom shelf and the bulkhead where these were going to be installed thin pencil line on both sides of the plywood dividers.

➤ Remove the dividers and drill three holes on the bottom shelf and two on the bulkhead where the centres of the dividers were to be installed. The holes were countersunk on the opposite sides.

➤ Coat the plywood dividers with glue and held them in place. Drill pilot holes and then installed 1 1/2" #6 screws to permanently mount the dividers.

➤ In the next step install a series of ¼ inch wide wood strips to provide support for the plywood top of the cabinet.

- Cut the cabinet top from ½ inch plywood and this was cut to fit. Initially cut to 69 1/2" wide and 24" deep, but maybe the cabin dimensions were not perfect so you had to trim a little in width to get it to fit. Also, note the hole with wires coming through it.
- Glue and then glue the top cabinet legs with two center dividers (1 inch pegs were used).
- Cut the top and bottom cherry frames and also cut the remaining 4 cherry stiles from the same stock as the galley cabinets. Use Pocket holes and glue to create the frame. Use a small hand plane to shave the frame down a fraction of an inch in width.
- Took some wood off both sides with the upper right-hand corner being the most difficult to fit. There will be a slight wave in the interior wall.
- Unlike the galley, these cabinets are deep enough. Use the Kreg Jig to drill pocket holes in the plywood and attach the face frame with screws and glue it.
- With the cabinet front in place, framed in the space above the cabinet. It was about 12" at the front and 6" at the rear where it intersects with the bulkhead. Left open the space to hold pillows, sleeping bags, and other stuff. Install the framing to help hold the lightweight stuff in place.
- Run a cable made out of 1/4" x 3/4" cherry that is used to cover the wires that were run through the cabin walls and drop down to the "wiring closet". Cut the cable run to fit and glued in place once the electrical wiring is in place.

FOR MAKING CABINET DOORS

➤ Now it's time to make the cabinet doors, installation of the doors, and creation of the drawer for the interior cabin.

➤ Like the face frames in the prior step, start with 4/4 cherry boards - rip, join, and plan the rough dimensions needed for the cabinet doors - ¾ inch thick, 2 inch wide, and various lengths.

➤ Then sort these boards through and made 18 stiles upright portion of the doors. Cut about 1 inch longer than plan the finished doors to be to enable trimming during door construction.

➤ Left the rails as longer boards at this stage so you wouldn't be running a 6 inch long board across a table saw dado head or across a router bit.

➤ Rout all the cherry boards with a quarter rounds bit to take both edges off the front of the boards.

➤ Carefully inspect the boards. Determine the inner and outer door edges for each board and mark the inner edge for the dado cut.

➤ Set the dado head on the table saw to remove 3/8" of material in-depth and 1/2" in width on each board.

➤ Sand all the boards on a belt sander at this stage.

➤ The next step was to cut the rails and stiles to size with the miter saw. Made 4 interior doors.

➤ Once the miters cut then laid out each future cabinet door (face down in pieces) and marked left/right and cabinet position (door

1, 2, 3, 4) and then measured, marked, and drill the holes for the hinges.

➤ Then assemble the rails and stiles for each door. Glue on the common miter edge and 1 1/2" brad nails to hold the door in place while the glue dried. Do the assembly on a piece of granite leftover from another project so you would have a nice flat table.

➤ While the doors dry, cut the ¼ inch cherry plywood to fit in each door. When the door dry, apply a thin line of glue to the dado cuts in each door frame and press the plywood in. Place something heavy on the plywood to hold it in place while they dry.

➤ Install the hinges on all the doors and dry to fit in the cabinet frames.

➤ Once the dry and fit process was completed then removes the hinges and drills the doorknob holes. Give each door a final hand sanding.

➤ After hand sanding the doors then seal them and let dry. Lightly sanded again and sealed it.

➤ Install the hinges and doorknobs. Also, install the doors on the cabinet frames.

➤ Now it's time to make a big drawer in the interior of the cabin that is a box on drawer slides. Use 75# drawer slides rather than the more inexpensive slides that are typical in-home use.

➤ Start the drawer with 2 - 1/2" x 12" x 24" and 2 - 1/2" x 12" x 18" pieces of plywood.

- Set up the table saw with a 3/8 inch dado blade and cut each piece of plywood. Receive a ¼ inch deep dado cut ½ inch in from the edge of the wood.
- Measure a piece of ¼ inch plywood left over from the cabin wall to fit the bottom of the drawer.
- Glue the front and back pieces to the side pieces. Don't forget to put the drawer bottom and use brad nails to hold it together.
- Next mount the drawer slides on the drawer and the cabinet. Insert the drawer into the cabinet mounted slides. Create a 1/16 inch shim and mount it on the back right cabinet slide to fix it.
- Finally cut a piece of the ¼ inch cherry plywood and glue that onto the draw to provide a nice drawer face and sealed the drawer face.
- Now the Cabinetry is finalized.

The Kitchen - Room with a view

Cut the sheets for the tabletop which is 24 inches in length and the stand is 21 inches high, both 46 1/2 (and 581/2 for 5x8) inches in width. Move the stand 22 inches from the floor, place the table over the stand, and centre it on the stand. Line up the stand and drill to anchor in the walls. Now do the same with the table stand. Now for the shelf in the bedroom and in the kitchen, cut two pieces of plywood 8 "high and 46 1/2" wide.

Run the first Piece of Plywood straight up then down and flush with the back of the interior wall. This piece acts as the wall for the shelves. Screw a wall to each side of the exterior walls. Then take a second 46 1/2 "8" piece (or 581/2 for 5x8) and centre it.

Secure it and drill into the exterior walls. First join the two 8 inch pieces like making a "T ", then secure into the side walls. Once you've finished this part of the build you can now install your railings in the bedroom and the kitchen. Make a good layer of wood glue or contact cement then it works fine. Don't try screwing these railings in, they will split.

Building the back hatch

- The back hatch was the most complex part of the entire construction process. Because of the size, it needed to be rigid during transportation and to be able to support its weight when open and it put stress on the hinge.
- A special order hinge was designed to prevent leakage.
- To start the back hatch use a pair of dividers and traced a 2 inch line along the back of the cabin from the point to the floor of the cabin.
- Once the 2 inch line on both sides of the cabin then uses the trusty saber saw to carefully cut the two exterior hatch pieces from the cabin.
- Take two shapes as the guides and drew 5 more arcs on a piece of ½ inch plywood.
- Cut about 1/8 inch outside the guidelines for all the arcs to leave wood for final contouring of the hatch.
- Once all the arcs were cut sandwiched the 5 arcs and the two cabin pieces together and clamped them in multiple locations. It took a while to align all 7 pieces up. Cut all by hand with the help of a saber saw so unfortunately there were be no variations.
- The next step was to drill three holes through the assembly and to insert some threaded rod through the holes and to tighten then all together.
- This provided a very solid unmovable assembly that could be taken to a belt sander and the interior and exteriors were sanded

to provide a smooth common face on the interior and exterior of the arcs.

➢ The cabin walls where the hatch pieces were also sanded (carefully) to maintain the consistency of the arcs and to provide sufficient space for the gaskets that would be mounted on the hatch and cabin to prevent water intrusion.

➢ Made 3 - ¾ inch x 2 inch x 72 inch oak struts - one for the bottom of the hatch frame, one for the top. From the top and bottom cut ¾ inch the curved hatch struts. The remaining strut was cut to fit inside the two exterior struts and glued/screwed to the top oak strut and the exterior studs. When framing the cabin struts use double oak struts for installing the hinges for strength.

➢ Also cut ¾ inch of an inch from the bottom of each of the 5 interior struts and cut 1 ½ inch from the top of each strut. Don't cut a full ¾ inch and 1 ½ inch initially. Made each cut a little for the final fit size to give some leeway in case something didn't fit right. Once strut fit each and verified then you see how much additional cut was required.

➢ The 5 interior arcs were then put into the hatch frame and adjusted until they were spaced 12 inch apart centre to centre. This resulted in the wall arcs and the first arcs in from the wall being less than 12 inch apart.

➢ With the interior arcs in place drill the pilot holes from the bottom struts into the arcs and using 2 ½ inch #8 screws on top and 1 ½ inch #8 screws on the bottom to mount the interior arcs.

➢ Next cut the arc cross braces. Use firing lath (all the leftover pieces from framing the cabin roof were used here). Cut the firing lath to 11 ½ inch for the interior locations and less for the struts between the hatch edge and the first arcs in on the left and right. Made 36 of these struts initially then added a few additional in to provide support for the hatch latches and mounting points for the LED floodlights.

➢ It was very important to square the frame up at this stage and to remain aware of the need to keep the hatch frame square throughout the rest of the framing process.

➢ Installation of the arc cross braces was done using 1 ½ inch brads in the finish nailing. Coat each end of the cross braces with glue, position it, and drive 2 brads into each end. Each brace was offset from the one adjacent to it so it could get the nails straight. Put spacers between every arc at the top and bottom of the hatch and nailed/glued these in place.

➢ Once the frame was dry installed the hinge and dry fit the frame to ensure everything was good to go for the remaining construction.

➢ The next thing is the installation of the hatch latches. Purchase marine-grade hatch latches and cut a couple 3" long pieces of angle iron to attach to the cabin walls. Latch installation was accomplished following the directions that came with the latches and using scrap pieces of the 1/8" plywood to get the spacing right on the outer shell of the hatch. These needed to be positioned and framed out so they could be mounted to latch the hatch down securely.

➢ Before beginning to cover the hatch with plywood ran the wiring (two circuits) for the LED strip lights and the LED floodlights. One floodlight was positioned so it would shine on the stove and one was positioned to shine where the dish sink was to be located.

- The wires come out the top left corner of the hatch and are terminated with connectors that enable the removal of the hatch.
- The final step for constructing the hatch is installing the plywood coverings. Use the remainder of the 1/8" plywood for both the external and internal sides of the hatch.
- The external side of the hatch was covered first using a full sheet to cover most of the hatch and some smaller pieces added at the bottom. This was glued and then held in place with brads until dry.
- The interior of the hatch was covered with the remaining pieces of 1/8 inch plywood.
- The seams and all the nail heads were all sealed with bond and sanded down to be flush.
- After that again seal with marine grade epoxy and coated with white primer inside and out.
- When the primer was dry, strips of gasket material were applied to both the cabin arc and the hatch to prevent water from migrating into the galley area.
- The hinge was heavily coated with OSI caulk and mounted on the cabin body (it had been dry fit earlier with the hatch) with screws.
- The hatch side of the hinge was heavily coated with caulk and the hatch was moved into position with aid from the apprentice. The hinge was then screwed tightly down.
- The caulk took about 3 days to dry sufficiently to trim it back with a drywall knife.

- The hatch lights were installed and the wiring was connected and there was light!
- The final step was the creation of a way to hold the hatch open. You can purchase two 1/2" dowels and made a couple of blocks of wood 3/4" x 1 1/2" x 2" that was partially drilled through with 3/4" fastener bits and mounted on the interior of the hatch just inside cabin walls.
- Take two pieces of 1/8" x 1/2" aluminium bar and wrapped them around the dowels to make mounting points on the galley prep top these were attached to the galley walls.

Insulation

Now that you've finished the interior and electrical parts, you can isolate what now looks like a teardrop pendant. Take 4 x 8 sheets 1 1/2 "thick. Measure each area and trim it to size. Once you are done with the insulation. You may also want to use blue leather. It is a self-adhesive composite membrane made from a rubberized SBS -Asphalt compound completely laminated with a blue high density polyethylene film, the membrane is specially designed to adhere to the prepared substrate and provide a highly effective sealing barrier.

WARNING

Never sleep in a drop-shaped harness without an open window or vent to let in fresh air. The volume of air in a tear prevents you from breathing all night. This could be your last one if it is sealed too tightly.

Sealing / Finishing the Interior

➤ The interior of the trailer has solid cherry trim. Trim is consisted of about 80 feet of 1/8" x 3/4" flat trim. For making trim join 1 edge of a 6' to 8' long 3/4" cherry board followed by ripping 3/16" from the board. Join the ripped edge of the board. Repeat the ripping and join until you had all the flat trim. Sand the 3/16" trim on both sides with a belt sander which brought the thickness down to close to 1/8". This thickness was chosen because of the tight curves in the cabin and the desire to hide the edges where the interior plywood and interior walls came together. The individual pieces of the 1/8" interior ceiling plywood joints came together.

➤ Also, make about 80 feet of 1/2" quarter round cherry trim by ripping 5/8" square trim; running it through a plan on the two ripped sides to get 1/2" square trim. After that routed with a quarter round bit to get 1/2" quarter round trim.

➤ Glue and use small finish brad nails to mount the trim. Mount the 1/2" quarter round on top of the 1/8" flat trim along the edges where the ceiling and the walls met. To create a 1/2-inch quarter-round for a proper fit along a curved roof line, cut grooves in the back of the quarter-round so that a row of 2 to 3-inch pieces can be bent, or cut and joined together with a miter saw Curve.

- Install quarter round on the top and bottom of the shelf at the front of the cabin, where the shelf met the interior ceiling.
- Coat the entire interior with two coats of polyurethane. Lightly hand sanded the first coat with the help of 220 grit sandpaper after it had dried.
- After the interior was sealed then install the cabinet doors. Mount the cabinet doors for fit checks much earlier in the process and sealed earlier in the process. The cabinet doors were finished products when they were installed.
- Then the next step is to work on the floor. Always work on the floor at last because in this way you didn't get to drop tools or scuff the floor while still trying to finish other parts of the construction.
- For finishing the floor, it consists of laying ¼ inch cork underlayment on the floor and halfway up the front wall. Select cork for its insulation and sound reduction properties rather than using newer man-made materials. Using the cork as the front wall headboard it helps to deaden sound reflected within the cabin and sound coming in from exterior sources.
- You get one chance to lay everything outright, so measure and dry fit the cork and plan the installation process by dry running the installation!!!
- Use a quart of contact cement and a roller to apply it to the cork and let it dry. Cover the floor and wall with the same adhesive and let it dry also.

➢ Once the cork was down, install the wood flooring. The hard part of laying the wood floor was pretty narrow so you had to rip several floorboards which were a dusty process.

➢ After the floor was down, install cork for the headboard and install the final trim around the entire floor covering up the floor edges with ½ inch quarter round held in place with finishing brads.

➢ Install coat hooks in convenient locations within the cabin.

➢ Also, place curtains to block light. Sew hooks on each curtain. Mount self-adhesive curtains above the doors and around the roof vent to block light.

Skin the trailer (Optional)

When installing thick 4 x 8 1/8 '' (STD) fibreboard, make sure you start with the hinge forward. You'll come up short, and it's easier to hide the extended piece at the front of the trailer instead of trying to hide it on the roof.

An 8-inch checker plate trim and a trailer tongue hide it quite nicely much better than trying to add a piece of aluminium on the roof to cover it up.

Note: As you install your hardboard, you may want to temporarily install your hinge at the same time, to keep everything aligned. Also, place some shims on either side of the galley door to stay in place.

Aluminium Extrusion

Now is the time to put everything together with the walls, the roof, the doors, the hinge, and the trim. If you're doing aluminium walls, there is no need for contact cement. First, set your aluminium walls in place and then install your doors. It's now that you want to make sure your aluminium walls and door cut-outs are lined up properly. Now fix the bottom of the walls with an aluminium strip. Once the floor and doors are in place, take a drop of sealant all over the roof and wall seam from top to bottom, then screw the extruded trim on.

Try changing sides every 4 or 5 screws, always making sure the roof is in line with the walls. Once you've screwed in all the siding, press down on the PVC to hide the screws.

Manufactured doors are easy to install. They come with an outer ring that fits the inside of the teardrop trailer wall and you slide the door through the ¾ inch wall by screwing the doorframe and ring together, but they are not cheap.

Hurricane Hinge

The hurricane hinge is a 2-Piece Extruded Aluminium Mill Finish. Line the galley roof and door; Screw in the hinge and make sure your door is properly aligned with some temporary standoffs that keep it in place. Install a second extruded trim on the opposite side for extra support. Make sure you use lots of caulking under the lip of the hinge and outside.

This is where you have the best chance of water leakage on your trailer. Water tends to create a pool on the top of the roof and seeps into anywhere it can find a hole. After you have installed your hinge, remember that it is two separate pieces. In other words, the hinge can slide back and forth, and if you're not paying attention it can go out of alignment.

Install Galley Hardware

Now it's time to install the latch for your rear galley door. Decide where the rear door you want it. Use an 8-inch strip of checker plate for the base of the door, and drilled a hole centered directly above the checker plate. Also, use a 2 position rear galley lid latch assembly.

Take 2 Point Latch, 1 Rear Deck "T" Handle Keyed, two 36" Rods that can be cut and bent to fit your application, and two Rod Mounting Brackets.

Once you install your hardware you need to line up two holes in the sides of the walls. This part is a little tricky. When you close the door, you can't see where to line up the holes.

Galley Hatch Seal

Use an Improved thick Vinyl boat trim and Aluminium Rub rail in replacement of the Original PVC. To embed vinyl into aluminium siding, it must be boiled until soft. We take vinyl from boiling water and insert the insert into the siding. Drive carefully with a rubber mallet. Once cured, the vinyl becomes waterproof.

Gas Springs

Use 115 - 120 lbs gas springs depending on the weight of your rear galley door. Remember one thing, these doors are heavy, and with a couple of gas springs properly attached, it will make your door opening a lot easier.

If you decide to install gas springs and don't want any issues in the future, then bolt the brackets to the wall and install the bolts right through the entire wall, either with a woody or aluminium sidewalls. If you just screw the brackets to the walls, you will find the constant opening and closing of the door will weaken the screw holes, and eventually, the brackets could come right off.

Fenders, Tires, and Rims

Let's start with the fenders. If you plan on doing a lot of travelling you don't want to go any smaller then use a 12-inch tire. 8 Inch can handle your trailer, but the smaller the tires the more rotations produce. This means your wheel bearings get warmer.

When it comes to the rims, bolt pattern, and fenders it's just a matter of choice and how much you want to spend on it. From this point on, it's all a matter of making the teardrop trailer your own. Also, keep a spare tire and the tools to change it.

Benefits of camping in teardrop trailers

Teardrop camping has been around since the 1920s, and it became increasingly popular in the immediate aftermath of World War II when raw materials were plentiful and soldiers returning home looked for more convenient ways to take families on the trek. Over the years, however, the pendants got bigger and more luxurious, and the rift went out of style.

They still had fans, but more and more people were moving to big tent trailers and big caravans. In recent years, tears have grown in popularity as more and more people are rediscovering these wonderful little pendants and their benefits. The teardrop style trailer has several advantages that people sing praises for.

➤ **Operating costs:** Teardrops are very light and easy to tow behind a small vehicle. It can be very economical and much cheaper to transport than a large van.

➤ **Campsites:** Trees can devastate (and damage) large caravans and therefore often get stuck on flat, barren campsites. Since tears are small, they can be used in much more scenic places.

➤ **Outdoors:** Tears encourage you to be outdoors and enjoy the outdoors, while caravans encourage you to be indoors and enjoy luxury.

- ➤ **Outdoor storage:** Tears fit easily in the garage. Caravans often require external storage, which can be very expensive.

- ➤ **Cost:** Tears are much cheaper to buy than large caravans.

- ➤ **Maintenance:** The larger the rig, the more maintenance you will have and the more money you will spend on it. Tears are very easy to use and do not require much maintenance.

- ➤ **Resale value:** Teardrops retain their resale value very well when compared to folding tarpaulin trailers and caravans.

- ➤ **Ultra Towable:** Teardrop trailers are the smallest RV trailers in the world. Most of the drops are between 1.5 and 2 m wide and almost never longer than 3.5 m, which means that little space is required. You don't need a heavy vehicle to tow your average teardrop trailer. Since the tear takes up very little space and is not very heavy, it can be pulled by almost any type of vehicle, including compact cars and even motorcycles. You don't need mirror extensions as the width of the trailer (including the fenders) is the same width as the average car. So it's very easy to manoeuvre and you don't need to remember more about the trailer than the car. Chances are, anything in your garage is capable of pulling out the teardrop suspension.

- ➤ **Aesthetics and Functionality:** Teardrops are some of the most popular bespoke models, and some of these bespoke rides are great. The wooden facade, the retro design and much more make the droplet pendants the most attractive pendants on the market. You also get a feature. A well-built blob trailer offers plenty of sleeping space for two or maybe three people and also has great kitchens attached. Some people have their tears equipped with electricity, air conditioning, televisions, etc., others look more rustic with simple sleeping areas and a galley.

> **Low fuel consumption:** the aerodynamic shape and low weight of the droplet trailer minimizes fuel consumption. Basically + 20% of your car's average fuel consumption.

When camping, you need to get closer to nature and not move the living room to a new location. Outdoors, it's easy to join in and enjoy for very little or no cost. Teardrop trailers offer the convenience of a caravan but, like a tent, bring us closer to nature. In fact, over the years, we had all the necessary equipment (tents, chairs, air mattress, stove, lanterns, and more) needed for camping, but we rarely camped because it was too tedious to load / unload, set up and take out this is. Remove your car and tent after each ride. After a while, it got tiresome. With our trailer, we can charge, pair and drive away in minutes and head to our favourite campsite. Once at the campsite, the construction of the camp takes every 10 minutes and we enjoy nature.

Disadvantages of teardrop trailers

There are also some disadvantages of the teardrop trailers some of them are listed below:

➢ **Teardrop trailers are small** – Tiny life is fashionable, but it's not for everyone, even if it's just a weekend getaway. Teardrops offer a lot in terms of versatility and flexibility, but living spaces can be cramped and storage space is limited.

➢ **Teardrop trailers have no bathrooms** – These systems often lack bathrooms. So when you are travelling without a portable pot, outdoor shower, or other accessory, you must rely on the use of campgrounds or proper disposal of your trash in the wild.

➢ **Teardrop trailers don't have indoor kitchens** – Some teardrops have an outdoor kitchenette at the rear of the rig. If the weather permits, or if you're just used to cooking outside, an open kitchen can't be a disadvantage. Trying to cook in inclement weather (e.g. raw eggs?), However, may not be ideal.

While drop trailers may not be for all RV enthusiasts, they are a great option for people looking for a low maintenance and tow bar.